# ROBERTS' RULES

## OF

# LESBIAN LIVING

## Shelly Roberts

# ROBERTS' RULES

## OF

# LESBIAN LIVING

## Shelly Roberts

Spinsters Ink
Duluth, Minnesota

Roberts' Rules of Lesbian Living © 1996 by Shelly Roberts

Spinsters Ink
32 E. First St., #330
Duluth, MN 55802-2002

Production:     Charlene Brown        Jami Snyder
                Helen Dooley          Jean Sramek
                Joan Drury            Amy Strasheim
                Claire Kirch          Liz Tufte
                Lori Loughney         Nancy Walker

*Library of Congress Cataloging-in-Publication Data*

Roberts, Shelly. 1943–
    Roberts' rules of lesbian living / Shelly Roberts.
    p.    cm.
ISBN 1-883523-09-5
    1. Lesbians–United States–Humor. 2. Lesbianism–United States–Humor.
I. Title.
PN6231.L43R66        1996                                95-52256
818'.5402–dc20                                              CIP

Printed in the U.S.A. on acid-free recycled paper.

# INTRODUCTION

We make it up as we go along.

Lesbians have *always* made it up as we go along.

This is what I've seen so far. Thought so far. Puzzled out and figured out for myself.

Your mileage may vary.

— *Shelly Roberts*

It is never a good idea
to ask someone to marry you
*before* the first date.

Contrary to popular opinion,
tofu is *not* a food.

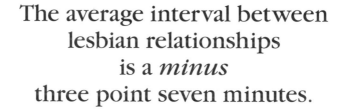

The average interval between
lesbian relationships
is a *minus*
three point seven minutes.

Your bumper sticker is
preaching to the converted.

It is much cheaper to say—
*"No, thank you, I have to
milk the bison this weekend"* —
now
than it is to break up
later.
It is not, however, easier.

"I love you."
is *not* a question.

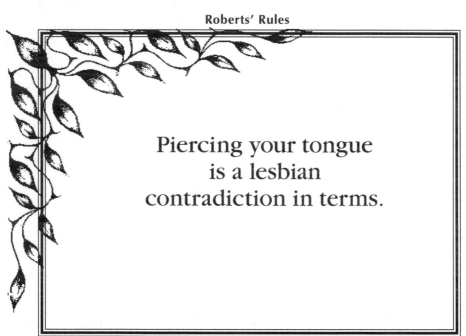

Piercing your tongue
is a lesbian
contradiction in terms.

Someone *will* mistake the triangle or rainbow on your car for a university parking permit.

Any friend in need of being
"fixed up" is way too broken
to be ready to date.

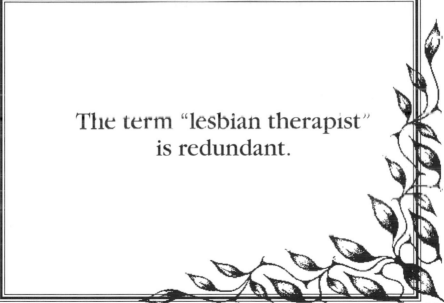

The term "lesbian therapist"
is redundant.

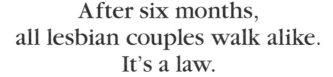

After six months,
all lesbian couples walk alike.
It's a law.

After one year,
all lesbian couples
will be wearing
at least one matching item.

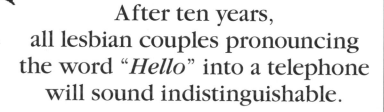

After ten years,
all lesbian couples pronouncing
the word "*Hello*" into a telephone
will sound indistinguishable.

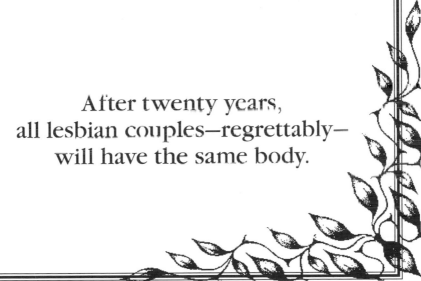

After twenty years,
all lesbian couples—regrettably—
will have the same body.

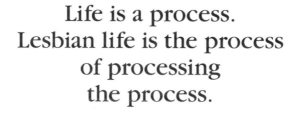

Life is a process.
Lesbian life is the process
of processing
the process.

Anybody who thinks
that being a lesbian
doesn't have something
to do with your mother
isn't paying
close attention.

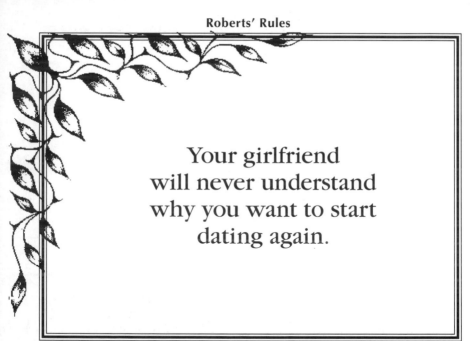

Your girlfriend
will never understand
why you want to start
dating again.

There's no such thing
as lesbian divorce.
There is only
thermonuclear war.
And then best friends.

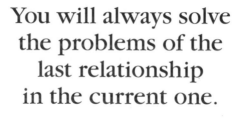

You will always solve
the problems of the
last relationship
in the current one.

It will not, however, help.

Just because you
never talk about any men
except your father
and brothers at work
does not automatically mean
that everyone there *surely*
must know you're a lesbian.

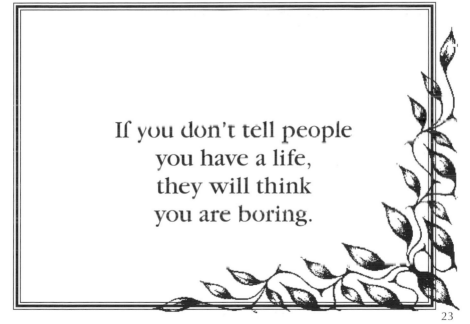

If you don't tell people
you have a life,
they will think
you are boring.

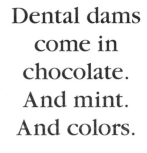

Dental dams
come in
chocolate.
And mint.
And colors.

Plasti-wrap is bigger,
but just comes in colors.

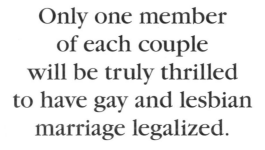

Only one member
of each couple
will be truly thrilled
to have gay and lesbian
marriage legalized.

Which one will vary
from day to day.

The only ex
that your current lover
will ever fully appreciate
is the one before at least the one
before her.

"No" is a complete sentence.

Lesbians don't hate men.

You must be thinking of
married straight women.

Not all nuns are lesbians.

Ditto flight attendants.

Not all members of the LPGA
are lesbians.

Ditto
professional tennis players.

Not all residents of
Key West, Little Five Points,
Park Slope, Northhampton,
Andersonville, Powderhorn Park,
Noe Valley, or Capitol Hill
are lesbians.

It's just wishful thinking.

Thanks to
Phil Donahue and PFLAG,
your mother no longer
automatically
believes she caused it.

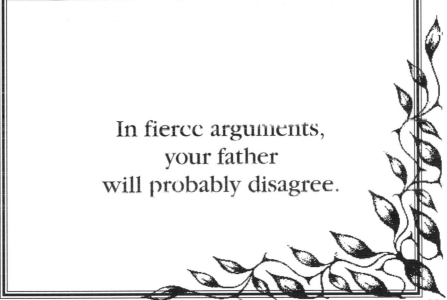

In fierce arguments,
your father
will probably disagree.

*Every* family,
if you include all the cousins,
has at least
one gay or lesbian member.

Your father will tell you
they're all on
your mother's side.

One-half of the gay or lesbian
businesses in your town
will be *out* of business
before the year's out.

The other half
will not believe that
you owe them a living.

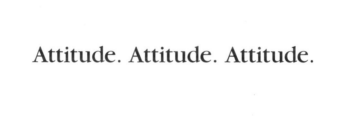

Attitude. Attitude. Attitude.

Attitude. Attitude. Attitude.

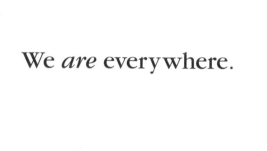

We *are* everywhere.

We *could* be anyone.

Your sisters and brothers
do know.

The word "lover" is
always more
than non-gay people
really want to know.

Your gaydar will only work
on half the population.

Gay men may be
of the same ilk,
but they are *not*
of the same species.

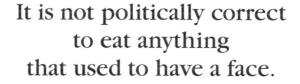

It is not politically correct
to eat anything
that used to have a face.

Or parents.

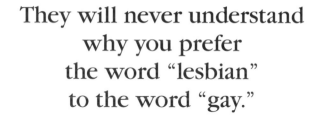

They will never understand
why you prefer
the word "lesbian"
to the word "gay."

They will get used to it.

Just like you did.

On a one-to-ten scale,
it is highly unlikely
that you really are
a five.

Your grandmother knows.

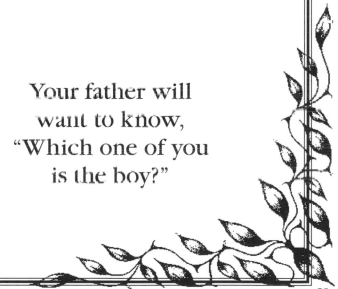

Your father will
want to know,
"Which one of you
is the boy?"

If you were married to a
man before you fell in love
with a woman, someone
will tell you that you're not a
"real" lesbian.

For a long time you will
believe she's right.
You'll get over it.

Sex changes everything.

If male homosexuals
are called "gay,"
then female homosexuals
should be called
"ecstatic."

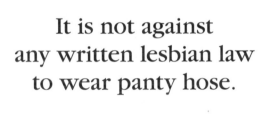

It is not against
any written lesbian law
to wear panty hose.

They just seem silly
under your softball uniform.

Dangling earrings
are not illegal.

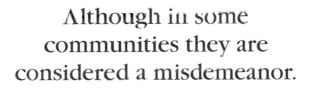

Although in some communities they are considered a misdemeanor.

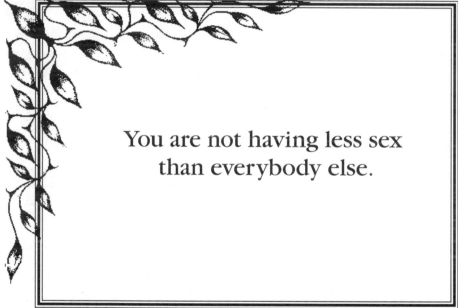

You are not having less sex
than everybody else.

Just less sex
than you used to.

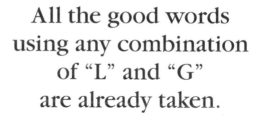

All the good words
using any combination
of "L" and "G"
are already taken.

Aren't you *glad*.
Raise the *flag*.
*Glom* onto the *glow*.
And don't *lag* behind.

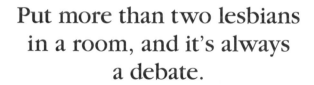

Put more than two lesbians
in a room, and it's always
a debate.

Any restaurant meal
attended by at least
four lesbians
automatically becomes
a Chinese dinner.

It is not impossible
to meet your next lover
in a bar or through
a personal ad.

Unlikely. But
not impossible.

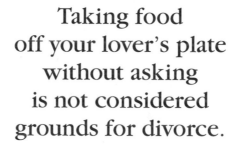

Taking food
off your lover's plate
without asking
is not considered
grounds for divorce.

For the first three years,
it's considered fair trade.

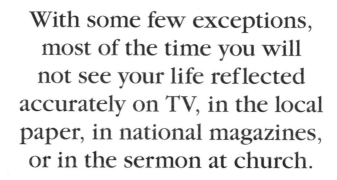

With some few exceptions, most of the time you will not see your life reflected accurately on TV, in the local paper, in national magazines, or in the sermon at church.

You're a woman.
This doesn't surprise you.

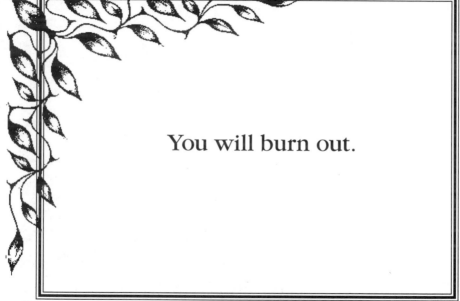

You will burn out.

You will come back.

You will burn out again.

You will come back again.

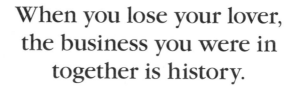

When you lose your lover,
the business you were in
together is history.

Er, uh, herstory.

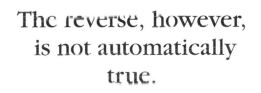

The reverse, however,
is not automatically
true.

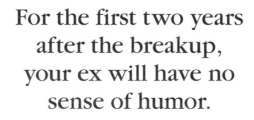

For the first two years
after the breakup,
your ex will have no
sense of humor.

She will believe
exactly the same of you.

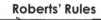

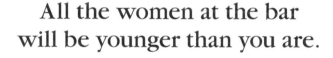

All the women at the bar
will be younger than you are.

Nobody else understands
drag queens either.

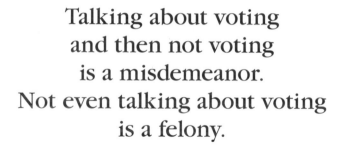

Talking about voting
and then not voting
is a misdemeanor.
Not even talking about voting
is a felony.

You should not consider
yourself lesbian-impaired
if you do not own
a chain saw.

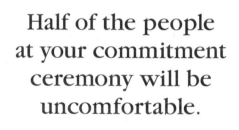

Half of the people
at your commitment
ceremony will be
uncomfortable.

Not counting your partner.

Your mother
will only complain
that you haven't
given her grandchildren
until you do.

Then she will find
something else.

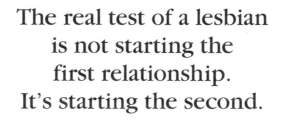

The real test of a lesbian
is not starting the
first relationship.
It's starting the second.

There is virtually
no difference between
Lesbian Standard Time
and the time your doctor's
appointment *actually* starts.

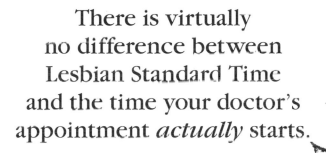

In the Olden Days, it was
believed there were
only *seven* lesbians in the
world, and the rest was done
with mirrors.

We know now
that there are *millions*
of lesbians...
but only seven
lesbian *haircuts*.

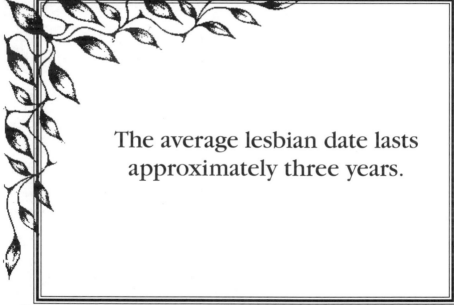

The average lesbian date lasts
approximately three years.

Parents should be reminded,
gently and often, that
"I love you *anyway*"
is not a compliment.

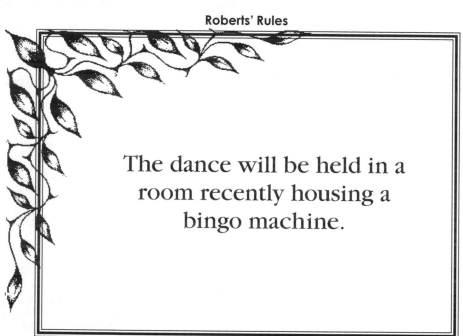

The dance will be held in a
room recently housing a
bingo machine.

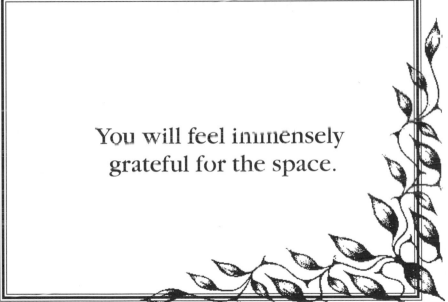

You will feel immensely
grateful for the space.

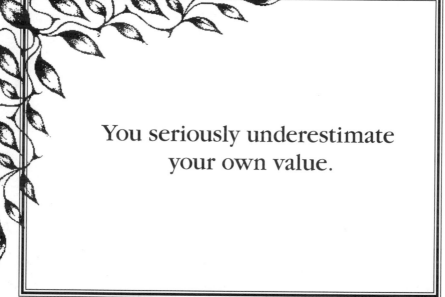

You seriously underestimate
your own value.

Again.

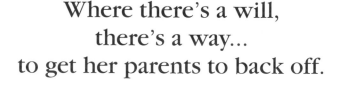

Where there's a will,
there's a way...
to get her parents to back off.

Do not,
under *any* circumstances,
put the credit card
in both your names.
(Years from now you'll thank me for this.)

Every lesbian brings a
a)   **toaster**
b)   **steam iron**
c)   **computer**
to each new relationship.

Without lesbians,
the Japanese would
go out of business.

Every lesbian brings a
    a)  cat
    b)  dog
    c)  parakeet
    d)  oxen
to each new relationship.

Without lesbians,
Bide-A-Wee, ASPCA, and
Animal Rescue Leagues
everywhere would
go out of business.

Four out of the next
twelve programs at the
local lesbian gathering group
will be about some kind
of financial management.

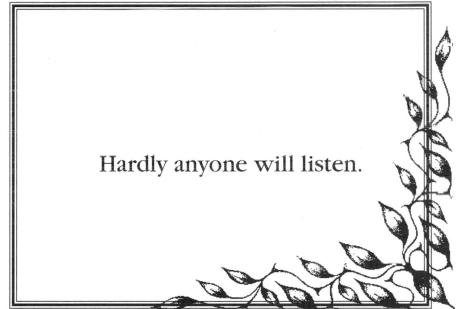

Hardly anyone will listen.

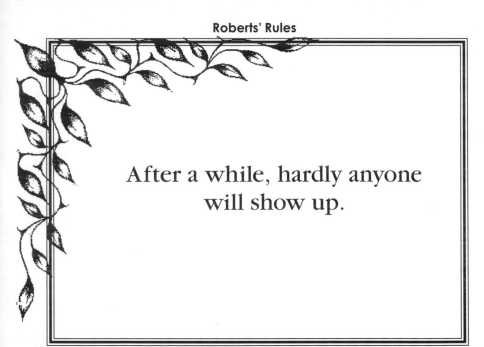

After a while, hardly anyone
will show up.

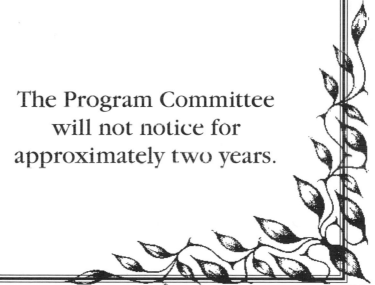

The Program Committee
will not notice for
approximately two years.

Your gynecologist doesn't
have to be a lesbian.

But it helps.

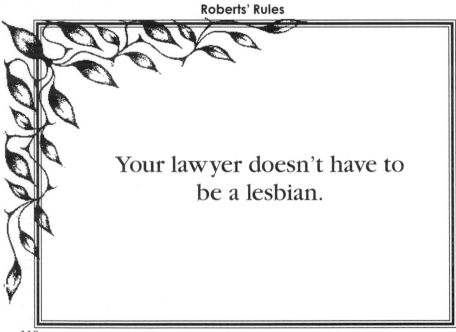

Your lawyer doesn't have to
be a lesbian.

But it helps.

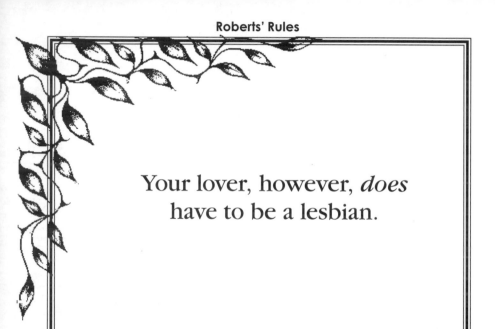

Your lover, however, *does* have to be a lesbian.

It's required.

Straight women are envious.

Especially the married ones.

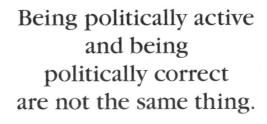

Being politically active
and being
politically correct
are not the same thing.

Lesbian humor
is not a
contradiction in terms.

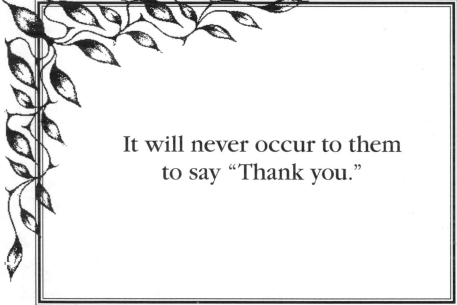

It will never occur to them
to say "Thank you."

Do it anyway.

There are only two kinds of
lesbians. Those who have
been to the Michigan
Womyn's Music Festival.
And those who shave their
body parts.

It is possible to spend
more time breaking up
than you actually spent
being together.

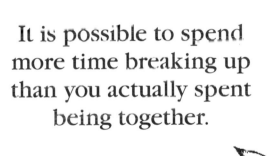

80% of the work
is always done by
20% of the lesbians.

Or more. And fewer.

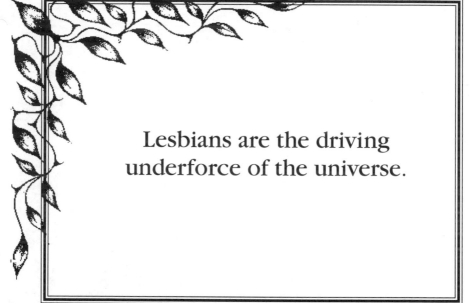

Lesbians are the driving underforce of the universe.

The reward you get
for solving a problem
in the lesbian community
is another problem.

It is never safe to assume
that whoever you're with
is straight.

And rarely accurate.

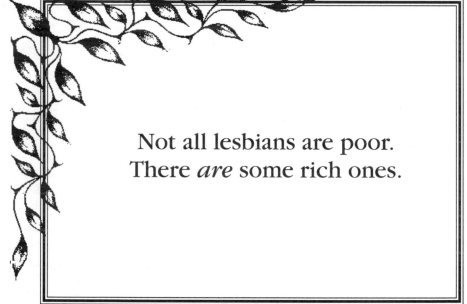

Not all lesbians are poor.
There *are* some rich ones.

They just don't usually go to
the same dances
as everyone else.

According to the
Bureau of Lesbian Statistics,
they treat you much worse
if they merely *suspect*
you're a lesbian,
than if you actually
tell them.

According to the *Lesbian Book of World Records*, if we moved out of New York City and Washington, D.C., they'd be empty.

To a lesbian, networking
is handing a business card
to another lesbian and
expecting the phone to ring.

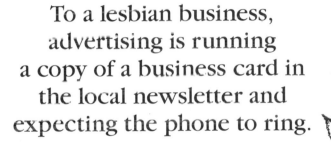

To a lesbian business,
advertising is running
a copy of a business card in
the local newsletter and
expecting the phone to ring.

To a single lesbian, dating is handing your telephone number to another single lesbian and expecting the phone to ring.

Lesbians, for the most part,
are an extraordinarily
optimistic group.

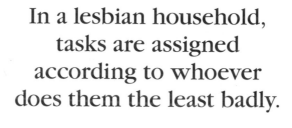

In a lesbian household,
tasks are assigned
according to whoever
does them the least badly.

Attitude. Latitude. Beatitude.

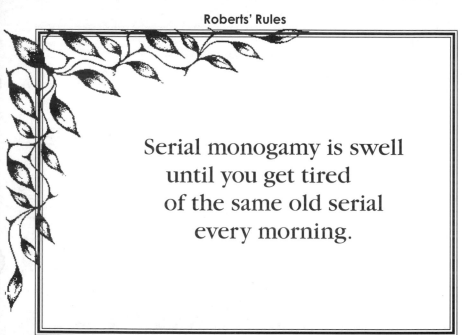

Serial monogamy is swell
until you get tired
of the same old serial
every morning.

No one will give you
domestic partner insurance
unless you ask for it.

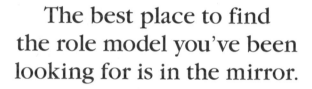

The best place to find
the role model you've been
looking for is in the mirror.

Sometimes the *only* place.

We are not only
their daughters and
their granddaughters,
we are also their mothers
and their grandmothers.

Also their aunts and
their great-grand aunts.

And their high school principal,
their attorney, their M.D.,
their company president,
and Her Honor, their mayor.

This often comes as more
of a surprise to *us*
than it does to *them*.

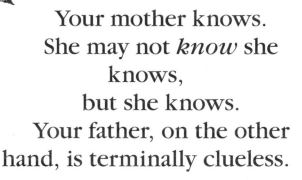

Your mother knows.
She may not *know* she
knows,
but she knows.
Your father, on the other
hand, is terminally clueless.

Or vice versa.

It is nearly impossible
for a lesbian to have
a best friend she has not
been previously married to.

Or won't soon be
married to.

If you want to know
four different ways to get from
Point A to Point B,
ask four different lesbians.

If you want a process,
ask them in the same room
at the same time.

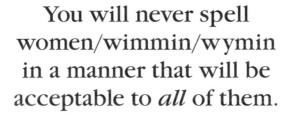

You will never spell
women/wimmin/wymin
in a manner that will be
acceptable to *all* of them.

Telling your mother that
you're happy
is *not* the same as
telling her you're gay.

Don't act normal,
act normally.

We are ten million women
waiting for someone else
to ask us to dance.

It can't be a sin.
We are not even
*in* the Bible.

Long-distance relationships
never reflect what
the relationship will look like in
the same house.

# Are there Hetero-sapiens?

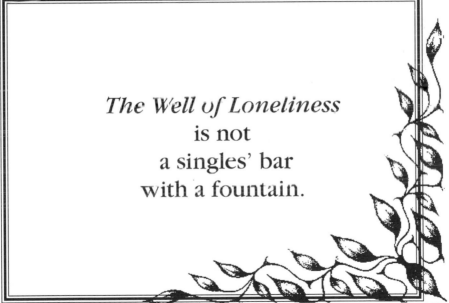

*The Well of Loneliness*
is not
a singles' bar
with a fountain.

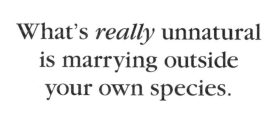

What's *really* unnatural
is marrying outside
your own species.

If you're starting a business,
don't depend on the community
for your soul support.

Bring home more flowers.

If you are planning
any activity at which you
don't want to be interrupted,
feed the cat first!

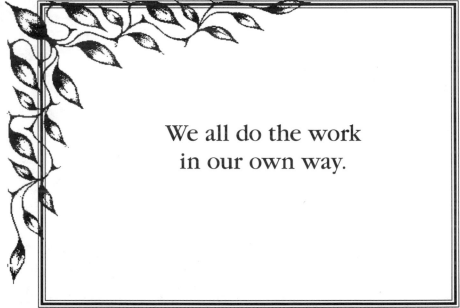

We all do the work
in our own way.

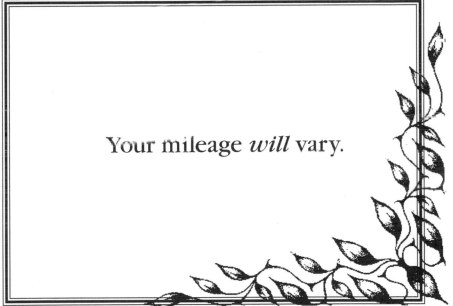

Your mileage *will* vary.

**Shelly Roberts** has been making up the rules every other week for years. Her nationally syndicated humor column, *Roberts' Rules,* reaches millions in gay and lesbian papers and magazines throughout the United States, Canada, Europe, and Asia. Shelly is also an in-demand speaker, and the author of a number of other books. Many of which are lesbian/gay. All of which are funny. Mostly on purpose.

**Spinsters Ink** was founded in 1978 to produce vital books for diverse women's communities. In 1986 we merged with Aunt Lute Books to become Spinsters/Aunt Lute. In 1990, the Aunt Lute Foundation became an independent, nonprofit publishing program. In 1992, Spinsters moved to Minnesota.

Spinsters Ink is committed to publishing novels and nonfiction works by women that deal with significant issues from a feminist perspective: books that not only name crucial issues in women's lives, but more important, encourage change and growth; books that help make the best in our lives more possible.

## Other Titles Available From Spinsters Ink

| | |
|---|---|
| *All the Muscle You Need,* Diana McRae | $8.95 |
| *Amazon Story Bones,* Ellen Frye | $10.95 |
| *As You Desire,* Madeline Moore | $9.95 |
| *Being Someone,* Ann MacLeod | $9.95 |
| *Cancer in Two Voices,* Butler & Rosenblum | $12.95 |
| *Child of Her People,* Anne Cameron | $8.95 |
| *Common Murder,* Val McDermid | $9.95 |
| *Considering Parenthood,* Cheri Pies | $12.95 |
| *Desert Years,* Cynthia Rich | $7.95 |
| *Elise,* Claire Kensington | $7.95 |
| *Fat Girl Dances with Rocks,* Susan Stinson | $10.95 |
| *Final Rest,* Mary Morell | $9.95 |
| *Final Session,* Mary Morell | $9.95 |

## Other Titles Available From Spinsters Ink

| | |
|---|---|
| *Give Me Your Good Ear,* 2nd Ed., Maureen Brady | $9.95 |
| *Goodness,* Martha Roth | $10.95 |
| *The Hangdog Hustle,* Elizabeth Pincus | $9.95 |
| *High and Outside,* Linnea A. Due | $8.95 |
| *The Journey,* Anne Cameron | $9.95 |
| *The Lesbian Erotic Dance,* JoAnn Loulan | $12.95 |
| *Lesbian Passion,* JoAnn Loulan | $12.95 |
| *Lesbian Sex,* JoAnn Loulan | $12.95 |
| *Lesbians at Midlife,* ed. by Sang, Warshow, & Smith | $12.95 |
| *The Lessons,* Melanie McAllester | $9.95 |
| *Life Savings,* Linnea Due | $10.95 |
| *Look Me in the Eye,* 2nd Ed., Macdonald & Rich | $8.95 |
| *Love and Memory,* Amy Oleson | $9.95 |

## Other Titles Available From Spinsters Ink

| | |
|---|---|
| *Martha Moody,* Susan Stinson | $10.95 |
| *Modern Daughters and the Outlaw West,* Melissa Kwasny | $9.95 |
| *Mother Journeys,* Sheldon, Reddy, Roth | $15.95 |
| *No Matter What,* Mary Saracino | $9.95 |
| *Ransacking the Closet,* Yvonne Zipter | $9.95 |
| *Roberts' Rules of Lesbian Living,* Shelly Roberts | $5.95 |
| *The Other Side of Silence,* Joan M. Drury | $9.95 |
| *The Solitary Twist,* Elizabeth Pincus | $9.95 |
| *Thirteen Steps,* Bonita L. Swan | $8.95 |
| *Trees Call for What They Need,* Melissa Kwasny | $9.95 |
| *The Two-Bit Tango,* Elizabeth Pincus | $9.95 |
| *Vital Ties,* Karen Kringle | $10.95 |
| *Why Can't Sharon Kowalski Come Home?* Thompson & Andrzejewski | $10.95 |

Spinsters Ink titles are available at your local booksellers or by mail order through Spinsters Ink. A free catalog is available upon request. Please include $2.00 for the first title ordered and 50¢ for every title thereafter. Visa and Mastercard accepted. Please contact us for author appearances and signings.

**Spinsters Ink**
**32 E. First St.**
**Duluth, MN 55802-2002**

**218-727-3222 (Phone)** **(Fax) 218-727-3119**
**(E-Mail) spinsters@aol.com**
**(World Wide Web) http://www.lesbian.org./spinsters-ink**